*"Community of Prayer* is no
ought to write. It is a sacri
Barkhauer, who has chosen. ... ᵍ.. . .. .... ....., .. ..., .......,
and strength to the work of generosity by God's people. He
reminds us that stewardship is a spiritual discipline. As such it
deserves a season of prayer and reflection, and listening to the
voice of God in our lives."
  —George Bullard, President of The Columbia
    Partnership and FaithSoaring Churches Learning
    Community

"Divine love, human generosity, flourishing earth, healthy
communities, God's realm, rest. Through daily meditations and
weekly deeper dives, Bruce Barkhauer connects the stewardship
dots. In so doing, he weaves a tapestry picturing God and God's
people in mutual giving that blesses the world."
  —Sharon Watkins, General Minister and President of the
    Christian Church (Disciples of Christ) in the United
    States and Canada, author of *Whole*

"So often the planners of the annual financial campaign do
little more than slap a bunch of financial figures in front of
the congregation and beg for money. Small wonder that congregations sometimes struggle financially. Bruce Barkhauer
puts a well-written, easy-to-read, practical resource in the
hands of churches to bring theological depth to the annual
financial campaign. On each of 29 days, the book offers a
theologically provocative meditation and a prayer around
themes of generosity, stewardship, and transformation. A
bonus: a 'going deeper' section for each week that an individual can pursue or that can spark a small group discussion. A
congregation whose members use these materials will deepen
spiritually, feel more connected, and become more generous."
  —Ronald J. Allen, Christian Theological Seminary

"For some congregations and their leaders, the anticipation of a financial stewardship emphasis is unfortunately not always the upbeat kind. In *Community of Prayer*, Bruce Barkhauer encourages making a financial commitment to the ministry of the church as an essential, transformative, and yes, celebratory moment! Daily meditations lead into four weekly emphases suitable for individual or group study. By engaging with Scripture and story, readers will gain a deeper understanding of stewardship that will lead to joyful and faithful generosity."

—Marcia Shetler, Executive Director/CEO, Ecumenical
    Stewardship Center

"Bruce Barkhauer has written a devotional guide that is a great gift to the church. These 29 devotionals will challenge us to ask, 'Who and what do we really worship?' They are not words to simply affirm that God loves us, but to wrestle with how much we love Him. The lure of this world is that stuff will save us and that possessing is the solution to our most pressing needs. How false!"

—J. Clif Christopher, President of Horizons
    Stewardship Company

"*Community of Prayer* offers daily reminders of the abundant love that calls us to live with hope — an especially powerful message in a popular culture warped by the fear of scarcity. Bruce Barkhauer's inspiring meditations and prayers ground the life of stewardship in a vision of God's gracious care that frees us to live each day with generosity, compassion, and a burning passion for justice. ... I am moved by this series of meditations. I believe you will be too."

—Richard Lowery, Christian Theological Seminary

# Community of PRAYER

## Stewardship Devotional

### BRUCE A. BARKHAUER

CBP

ST. LOUIS, MISSOURI

**CBPBooks.com**

Print: 9780827205444
EPUB: 9780827205451        EPDF: 9780827205468

# Contents

*To my families:*
*the one into which I was born by love,*
*the one into which I was embraced by choice,*
*the one into which I was grafted by faith,*
*and the Human One -*
*into which we are all conceived as*
*the precious children of God.*

# Introduction

At various times in the cycle of days we call the church year, we spend some extra moments in reflection and preparation. To welcome the Christ child, we have the four weeks of Advent. We sit quietly, not rushing too fast toward the stable, lest we run past the babe cradled in straw and miss the meaning of what "God with us" is all about. With the hope of Easter, and the meaning of both new and everlasting life on the horizon, we observe a period of reflection about the condition of our souls and of our world and our deep need for a word assuring us that nothing, not even death, can separate us from the love of God.

This work is directed toward an event that also requires preparation: The making of a financial commitment to the work and ministry of the church. If we want to be a full partner in the unfolding Realm of God around us, we cannot come to the moment of commitment with our best without being grounded in an understanding of stewardship.

Stewardship is not fundraising—it is a spiritual discipline. It is about responding with *our whole being* to the generosity of God. Stewardship impacts every aspect of life. How unfortunate for us that we have reduced this rich biblical concept to being simply about money. Perhaps the greatest sin of all is that we have made it about budgets and board reports instead of about a life-giving adventure and an invitation to discover deeper joy in discipleship.

What follows is a 29-day encounter with scripture and ideas about stewardship. Built into each day is a moment to pause for prayer. Designed into each week is a chance to "go deeper" with the concepts that the previous seven days have called to light. You can choose to do the "go deeper challenge" either by yourself or as a part of a small group. If you find yourself desiring to learn more, you can go "even deeper still" with the recommendations for readings, tools and other resources for each week.

Consider this book as preparation for a journey to a holy moment, in much the same way as you have used similar works to prepare for Christmas or Easter.

If you are using this resource in a congregational setting, your journey is likely heading toward a holy moment of financial commitment. This, then, is a part of your preparation, so that when the day arrives, you are able to make the best decision possible: one that reflects your hopes and desires; one that has been steeped in prayer and earnest reflection; one that is forged out of your love for (and being loved by) God. This is a choice with the potential to bring you great joy, and an opportunity to change the world.

My deepest appreciation to Brad Lyons and Chalice Press for seeing the value in this project, and to my wife and partner in life, Laura, who has not only encouraged me but has made certain that the words you read have clarity and meaning for a life of discipleship from the perspective of the pew. I also give thanks for Rev. Howard Goodrich, who many years ago placed the challenge to be a steward front and center in my ministry. He assured me that I could be generous and that I would never regret being so. He was right. Finally, I express gratitude for the good work the church has called me (and allows me) to do. It is a joyous thing indeed to be charged with helping to create a culture of generosity across our common life together. Thank you for being a part of that ministry by spending time in these pages. All of the royalties from this publication will directly benefit the Center for Faith and Giving.

*Bruce*

# Day 1

• • • • • •

# Stewardship Starts with WOW!

*How well you start often determines how well you finish.*

Two of our children were swimmers. A large part of their early training had to do with entering the water. Stroke and turn, endurance, and "dry land" conditioning was important, but in swimming if you don't get off the blocks well and make a clean entry into the water, you spend a great deal of energy catching the other swimmers. You have to start well if you hope to finish well.

The same can be said of stewardship. Where we embark in our understanding makes a difference as to whether or not we will discover the joy in giving and approach our true capacity for generosity. If we begin from a place of guilt or obligation, it is unlikely we will discover joy and gratitude. Starting from a place of wonder and "wow," however, opens the possibility that we can find delight and satisfaction in sharing and in our own practice of stewardship.

It starts with God rather than ourselves. The process of becoming a faithful steward is the realization that we are responding to what God has done, rather than seeking to generate a reaction from God. God has already blessed, already provided.

Genuine stewardship therefore finds the heart of its beginning in the "wow" of God. God, according to Genesis, looks upon the unfolding work of creation and says at the end of each day: "Wow – this is *good*!" All of it brings delight to the heart of the Divine One; such awe is the right way for us to start our stewardship conversation so that we can indeed end well.

**For Focus and Reflection:** What have been some "wow" moments in my life?

**Prayer:** *Lord, we thank you for good beginnings, fresh starts, and the first step in a new journey of discovery. Amen.*

# *Day 2*

●　●　●　●　●　●

# Delight Leads to Care

*God looked over everything that God had made; it was so good, so very good!* (Genesis 1:31, MSG)

We are learning some things as we grow older, including the reality that we have accumulated too much stuff. Recently our children watched us go through the "trash or stash" phase with our parents. Afterward they told us flat out, "We don't want your stuff." So we are choosing to do some sorting out now, rather than wait until our health or lifestyle choices force the issue. The questions we are asking regarding what to keep and what to let go are these: Is it necessary? Is it useful? Does it bring you joy?

"Does it bring you joy?" calls you to think about your relationship with your things. It is not a surprise then that what brings you joy is what you are most interested in protecting. Often these things are connected to people and relationships, or particular moments of meaning. These are the things that get bubble wrapped and boxed when stored. More often than not, you want to put them where they can be seen (and just out of the reach of your three-year-old grandson!) You want to preserve them and share them. Most of all, you want to experience them, because they bring delight.

When it comes to what God has created—you and me—as well as *all* the living things on this planet we share, you can find assurance in knowing that God wants to preserve and protect those things because they bring the Divine One joy. It is the nature of the relationship God has with you, and as you will discover, a form of stewardship.

*For Focus and Reflection:* What brings me delight that is worthy of sharing with others?

*Prayer: May I find in all living things the delight that you, O God, find in them and in me. Amen.*

2

# Day 3

• • • • • •

# Enough

*Abundance does not mean you get everything you want. It does mean you may have all that you need.*

The earth is teeming with life in the creation story. Winged things winging; swimming things swimming; creeping things creeping—stars fill the sky, every plant is weighed heavy with seeds, tree branches are laden with fruit. There is a remarkable abundance in the created order. There is no fear of scarcity. There is such a richness that everything can multiply without anxiety. The command and promise is given to "Prosper! Reproduce! Fill Earth! Take charge! Be responsible for fish in the sea and birds in the air, for every living thing that moves on the face of Earth" (Genesis 1:26, MSG).

No dread of running out. Enough, not only for today, but also for tomorrow—and the day after that, and the day after that! Things flourish because the system is designed that way. It is not designed for mindless exploitation. Care for all living things is a part of what it means to bear the image of God. Manage things here on the earth the way that God does in the universe so all can be well and whole. That is a good definition of stewardship.

When we fear that there won't be enough, we hoard. We take more for ourselves than we can use and in the process, something, or *someone* goes with less or none at all. We will never have all we want, but the Bible promises that we have what we need if we will but manage it well. It begs the question: How much is enough?

**For Focus and Reflection:** Do I have enough of what really matters? More than enough?

**Prayer:** *Lord, grant me eyes to see your abundance so that instead of closing my hand to hoard, I may open my hand to share. Amen.*

# Day 4

## ● ● ● ● ● ●

# Steward of (and from) the Earth

*The Lord God took the human creature and put him in the garden of Eden to protect and serve it.\* (Genesis 2:15)*

In Genesis chapters two and three, the author seeks to understand what it means to be human and the consequences as to the choice of living in the world on God's terms or our own terms. In the process of reminding us that choosing "our own terms" leads to fractured relationships across the whole spectrum of the cosmos, we also hear an affirmation about being a steward of the earth and a simultaneous beneficiary of God's provision.

We rightly think of the garden of Eden as paradise. But it is not so because of an absence of work, but because of the presence of God. (Remember that God would come and walk in the garden in the cool of the evening). Human beings have a vocation to live in such a way as for the garden (now all of the earth) to succeed. The humans care for the garden so that it thrives, and in return, the garden sustains us.

To care for the earth is not simply to be obedient to God as a steward, but by doing so we preserve our own best interest. The author of Genesis knows, and we forget at our own peril, that we are linked to the land. This means faithful stewardship involves choices that have a lower impact on the fragile sphere we call home. It suggests we should consider this in our consumption of the earth's resources.

*For Focus and Reflection:* What can I choose to do with less of for the sake of the earth?

*Prayer: God of creation, help me to care for all that you have made and to remember that by doing so, I am caring for myself and my neighbor.*

\*Rev. Carol Johnston, PhD, offers this helpful rendering instead of the traditional translation "Till and keep it."

# Day 5

• • • • • •

# A Weekly Reminder

*Sabbath is a weekly invitation—not to prohibition, but to permission—to enter into the fullness of life as a part of God's creation.*

Sunday as Sabbath, if you are old enough, conjures up images of closed businesses and quiet activities. It was a day for "thou shalt not." Don't work, don't go to the movies, don't play cards, don't miss church, and don't look like you are having fun! It wasn't all bad. For many, Sunday meant family dinners when relatives dropped in, and a slower pace to interrupt the rhythm of the work week.

Sabbath is more than what *not* to do. The seventh day of creation stands alone to remind us that we are not the Creator. The world does not exist because of our frenetic activity and our mindless busyness. Each week there is a reminder that we are the *created,* a part of something wonderful and awesome that is beyond our own clever crafting or industrious labor.

The entire cosmos is a gift—us and everything in it—close at hand or light years away. It is chaos brought to order by a Divine Word spoken. The result is a system of provision and abundance so magnificent that you only have to work six days and yet there is supply and produce for seven.

**"Work six days and do everything you need to do. But the seventh day is a Sabbath to God, your God. Don't do any work"** (Exodus. 20:10, MSG). Permission not to work. A command of God not to try to cram eight days into seven. A promise again of enough and an invitation to dare to trust God.

*For Focus and Reflection:* Where and how in my life do I take time to rest and catch my breath?

*Prayer: Holy One, may I come to rely more on your promise of provision. Amen.*

# Day 6

• • • • • •

# What Is This?

**God said to Moses, "I'm going to rain bread down from the skies for you."** (Exodus 16:4, MSG)

What is this? A First Testament scholar has assured me that this is one way to translate the word *manna*. Inquisitive? Exclamatory! Surprise or Shock? It is all in the way you read it. If you remember the story, any or all of these might be accurate.

After the miracle at the Red Sea you might have thought the people were really going to trust that God had their backs. They sure were happy standing on the seashore watching Pharaoh's chariots drown. But in no time at all the Back to Egypt Committee is having meetings in the parking lot.

They are hungry, and of all things, they start to have selective memory about how they "had their fill" in Egypt. So God tells Moses to get the people ready because the Wonder Bread truck is about to deliver. Manna—bread from heaven—is coming. But take note: (1) The bread will be enough, no matter how big the family or how able-bodied the household members, everyone will get what they *need*; (2) The bread will spoil if you take too much, if you aren't too sure about tomorrow and want to grab a little extra. It turns to worms. Yuck. That is, of course, with the exception of the day before the Sabbath. Then gather twice as much, and it won't spoil.

It is a test. Do you trust in the God who delivered you from slavery to deliver the goods, or not? Sabbath again becomes a proving ground for provision, and God is up to the task.

***For Focus and Reflection:*** What do I do daily that shows my trust in God's provision?

***Prayer:*** *God of daily bread, may I learn to trust you, as I pray: Our Father who art in…Amen.*

# Day 7

• • • • • • •

# A New Pharaoh?

*Don't ever forget that you were slaves in Egypt and God, your God, got you out of there in a powerful show of strength.* (Deuteronomy 5:15, MSG)

Beyond a day off, a promise of provision, or an opportunity to express trust in God, Sabbath proclaims that God is a liberator. The injunction to observe the Sabbath in Deuteronomy is tied directly to the deliverance from bondage in Egypt. *A slave does not get a day off.* Pharaoh, as the anxious taskmaster concerned only about brick tallies, can't stop production. These bricks are for supply cities, the hedge against the fickle gods of Egypt. In fear of scarcity, Pharaoh doesn't rest, and therefore neither do the people from the land of Goshen. The value of the Hebrews to Egypt is their ability to produce in the constant battle against insufficiency.

Enter the God of Abraham and Sarah, who is not concerned about having enough, and who, in the face of mounting manufacturing schedules, dares to take time to rest, confident in provision. This God is interested not in what the Hebrew children can produce, but in who they are. To take a day off is an invitation to remember who God is and what God has done. Imagine a God who breaks the yoke of the bondage of production and in whose service the burden is easy.

Isn't it strange then that we should choose to be busy all the time? That we work only to buy and consume with such vigor as to mask our fear of running out of what we need? Will having some *thing* or being constantly busy increase your self-worth or your value to others or to God? In your desire to acquire, have you chosen another Pharaoh?

*For Focus and Reflection:* God loves me for who I am, not what I produce. Is that mutual?

*Prayer: Help me in rest to discover your freedom. Amen.*

# Week 1 Going Deeper

*Resources for Individual Reflection or Group Discussion*

This week's focus was on the relationships between stewardship, creation, and Sabbath keeping. Clearly stewardship is about much more than money. The creation story infers that humans are to be stewards of the earth. We are to care for the earth the way God cares for the cosmos. We understand that this is what it really means to be created in the image of God. God richly provides for us in abundance, and we are to do the same within the web of relationships we share as the ones who have been created.

The creation narratives in Genesis 1 and 2 also seek to impart trust in God as the sustainer of what has been created. The fabric of the design includes ongoing provision. Sabbath (the seventh day of creation) reinforces this understanding by promising seven days of produce for six days of labor. Observing Sabbath creates the opportunity to exercise trust and to receive renewal by breaking the cycle of work. It is both remembering the power of God (defeating Pharaoh) and remembering that God's investment in us is *relationship*-based, not *commodity*-driven. It is never about what God can gain *from* us or what we can *produce* to satisfy the Divine.

**Read** Psalm 104. This is a beautiful reflection on the Genesis 1 poem. Can you see the similarities? Focus on verses 13–30. What does God do? What images or phrases captivate your imagination? Did you notice verses 27 and 28? What do they mean to you? How do they impact your understanding of being one who *receives* from God?

**Read** Leviticus 25:1–7. Notice that even the land gets rest. The land has its own agency within creation, giving it particular value and character of relationship. Numbers 35:34 states: "You shall not defile the land in which you live, in which I also dwell" (NRSV). Are we guilty of this? If so, how? In Leviticus 18:28, when urging Israel to keep the Law (of which this command is a part), the author suggests that the land itself "will vomit you out" (NRSV) if you don't follow these instructions. Are there places where the land is "vomiting us out" from its overuse or abuse? What can or should we do about that?

How do your choices as a consumer impact the earth? How are both people and resources exploited by certain aspects of our economic system? Should the church be concerned and look for ways to lessen the impact? How is this stewardship?

What are ways you might engage the congregation in this deeper understanding of stewardship as care for the earth? Could we do a better job with water or energy conservation, recycling, or even go so far as eliminating Styrofoam from the church kitchen? Regarding Sabbath, could we build more opportunities for rest and reflection in our common life together rather than just scheduling another meeting? Is it time for a retreat where we might talk less and listen more?

***For reading and further study:*** *Sabbath and Jubilee* by Richard Lowery (Chalice Press); *Sabbath as Resistance* by Walter Brueggemann (Westminster John Knox Press)

***Going Deeper Still*** – Read the Papal Encyclical by Pope Francis on care for the earth, *Laudato Si.*

Check out the "Community of Prayer" section on the Center for Faith and Giving website for additional resources, centerforfaithandgiving.org.

# Day 8

• • • • • •

# Temple Time

*Or didn't you realize that your body is a sacred place, the place of the Holy Spirit?* (1 Cor. 6:19, MSG)

Most of us would think of a temple as a place, not a person. The Apostle Paul, however, thinks a bit differently. You are a temple! You contain within you a spark of the Divine, a gift of God's presence in the Holy Spirit. In Jewish thought (remember Paul was a "Pharisee's Pharisee," deeply immersed in his tradition) you do not *have* a body so much as you *are* a body. The idea that you could somehow separate spirit, mind, and body would run contrary to Paul's experience. Judaism can talk separately about the three as traits, but in the end, they all come together as a homogenous package.

Paul is very concerned about purity and where we take the Spirit given that the Spirit goes where we go. Engaging in activities that God would approve of is a given. But something else is inferred in this passage. We are to offer our *whole self* as a sacrifice. Sacrifice here is not appeasement, but an invitation to mingle with the Holy. In the Bible, more often than not, sacrifice is bidding God to come—like putting out the welcome mat.

Give God the *very best* of what you have to offer in *everything* you do. To give your best, you have to be at your best. It is an invitation, and perhaps an admonition, to self-care. You cannot deploy the full potential of your gifts if your body is languishing. Sabbath rest, and yes, even eating well and exercising might be a part of your stewardship so that you are always at your best!

*For Focus and Reflection:* What can I do today that affirms and respects the gift of my body?

*Prayer: Lord, help me to see that in taking care of me, I can better serve you. Amen.*

# Day 9

• • • • • •

## Sharing a Secret

*One should think about us this way—as servants of Christ and stewards of the mysteries of God.* (1 Corinthians 4:1, NET)

You know a secret! You know the deep and mysterious ways of God. True, you don't know *all* about God and, no, it's not really a secret, but you do know the *most* important thing there is to know: *that God loves the world.* You know just how deep and powerful that love is because you have seen it in Jesus Christ. If you have heard the gospel and made a confession of faith; if you have been plunged into waters of baptism (with either a little or a lot of water); if you have received the seal of God's promise, the Holy Spirit, you know.

You know that in the life, death, and resurrection of Jesus is a proclamation that God's love for you (and the world), is stronger even than death itself. You know that the way of God is not violence or coercion, but gentleness and invitation. God *is a mystery* to a world that believes might makes right and where being the strongest is seen as an opportunity to impose your will on others. It is confusing to some that discipleship takes place more as God wooing us than commanding us.

But you do know, and so you are a steward of that message. A message that is to be shared rather than hidden. Far too often it is a well-kept secret. One friend of mine has suggested that at church, our version of keeping a secret is to only tell two or three people! Maybe that would help. To be a good steward is to share what you know.

*For Focus and Reflection:* What are some of the ways I might reflect God's Love for the world?

*Prayer: This little light of mine, I'm gonna let it shine… Amen.*

# Day 10

• • • • • •

# Steward of Grace

*"Like good stewards of the many colored graces\* of God, serve one another with whatever gift each of you has received."* (1 Peter 4:10, NRSV)

In relation to God, we think about grace as *unmerited favor*, which we call forgiveness. It is a grace we have *received*. We also recall in the Lord's Prayer that it urges us *to extend* grace to others. By doing so, grace is fully integrated into our experience and we become an expansion of Divine compassion turned loose in the world.

If you are a steward of the gospel, you are also a steward of grace. The gospel is a word of hope grounded in the redemptive love of God. It is about your worth to God and your place in community. Faith is never a solo act in the Bible. It is lived out within, and for the benefit of others. Each Easter I would remind my congregation that "Christ was not raised to get you into heaven, but to get heaven into you, and through you into the world." Our Easter celebration therefore is less about our salvation and more about how to be an answer to our own prayer: "...on earth as it is in heaven."

Elegance, kindness, blessing, beauty, and dignity can also define grace. Consider your assets. What do you do well? How can you enhance the work that God is doing in your midst? What are the *spiritual* graces you have been given that when you express them, enrich the community? Notice too that this is about diversity. And in that variety is Divinely inspired beauty. God does this through you when you act as a steward of what you have received.

**For Focus and Reflection:** What are my particular gifts that can make the world a better place?

**Prayer:** *God, help me to deploy my gifts as an agent of Your Realm. Amen.*

\*(NRSV says manifold graces – thanks to Rev Ron J. Allen for "many colored graces")

# *Day* 11

• • • • • •

# In God (god) We Trust?

*It seems that whenever I go to church they are always talking about money!*

Did you know that the Bible talks about money, or the derivatives of that idea, more than 2,500 times? More than love, grace, or salvation, concepts related to money, wealth, management, resources, buying, selling, lending, borrowing (well, you get the picture) dominate the sacred texts. If the church is talking about money—whether it is how to give it, how to save it, how to relate to it, how to use it, what money can do and what it can't—that is a church that is reading its Bible.

Many scholars believe that Jesus talked about money (or related concepts) perhaps as much as 60 percent of the time. Among the many things Jesus says about money (most of which can make us uncomfortable!) is that no one can serve two masters. "You can't worship two gods at once. Loving one god, you'll end up hating the other. Adoration of one feeds contempt for the other. You can't worship God and Money both" (Matthew 6:24, MSG). Jesus wants us to know that money makes a great servant but a lousy master. We can employ it as a tool for good. But relying on it to solve all our problems will end in disaster.

Despite all of money's power, it is ultimately less than God. Trusting in anything less than God will always disappoint, always lead to despair, and always end in death. Only God can give life, and life is not for sale. It does beg the question—do you believe more in what is printed on your currency or do you believe more in the money itself?

*For Focus and Reflection:* What have I elevated to the status of God?

*Prayer: Help me to choose wisely Whom (or what ) I decide to serve. Amen.*

# Day 12

• • • • • •

# Finding Your Heart

*For where your treasure is, there your heart will be also.* (Matthew 6:21, NRSV)

I confess that for years I understood this text as saying my treasure would naturally follow my heart. It was just the way I had heard it as a child. It was only as an adult that I came to realize the text says exactly the opposite. My heart will follow my treasure, not the other way around.

Jesus dares to say that your checkbook is a theological document. Look at your EFT statement at the end of the month and you will know what matters to you. Your money flows to what you love. Find your money and you will find your heart.

This would even apply to our congregations. The church budget is also a theological document. To what does our money flow? Are we caring for ourselves or are we seeking to impact the lives of others? Does our financial report show that we tithe as a congregation from the resources we receive to causes outside of our own concern?

In a season of stewardship preparation, you have to ask yourself, can you find your heart for God amidst the trail of debit and credit card transactions? Do the ledger entries demonstrate a concern for justice, a desire to bring wholeness, and the hope that no one should be without food, clean water and shelter? Or do they say something else?

In a season of stewardship preparation, you might ask yourself, where is your heart and is it where you hoped you would find it? Would a little more treasure invested in the Realm of God reflect what you would like the answer to be?

*For Focus and Reflection:* What do my checkbook and credit card statement tell me about my heart?

*Prayer: God, I desire my heart and my treasure to be less in conflict and more in line with you. Amen.*

14

# Day 13

• • • • • •

# Chill

*What I am trying to do here is to get you to relax, not be so preoccupied with getting so you can respond to God's giving. People who don't know God and the way God works fuss over these things, but you know both God and how God works. Steep yourself in God-reality, God-initiative, God-provisions. You'll find all your everyday concerns will be met.* (Luke 12:29–32, MSG)

Are you tempted to roll your eyes when Jesus says, "Don't worry about what you will eat or what you will wear"? Easy for you, Jesus. You can turn stones to bread; I have three kids in college! It seems to border on the irresponsible. Of course I worry. It is my job to put bread on the table and to clothe my family. I was taught to work for these things. Some nights I wake up and can't go back to sleep—worried about the *un*certainties.

And this is Jesus' point. There are *certainties*—God loves you and will provide for you. If we give ourselves over to the way of the Realm of God, if we practice stewardship with confidence, the community will never be without the basics it needs for life. And that includes you.

If God sees to the needs of the sparrows and wildflowers, surely (because you are valued more than these) God will take care of you. Spending all your energy (and sleepless nights) worrying about the basics robs you of the joy of life. Believing God doesn't care or notice steals your dignity. Like those who waited for manna in the desert, at some point you just have to trust God and relax.

*For Focus and Reflection:* What is my greatest anxiety and can I give it to God today?

*Prayer: Lord, trust is hard work, but being less anxious is more appealing than being afraid. Help me to rely on you more than myself. Amen.*

# Day 14

• • • • • •

# Why Give?

*Bring the full tithe into the storehouse, so that there may be food in my house, and thus put me to the test, says the Lord of hosts; see if I will not open the windows of heaven for you and pour down for you an overflowing blessing.* (Malachi 3:10, NRSV)

This passage has been used by some to say that we should give to God so that we will in turn be blessed. That "blessing" is almost always seen as material gain. It suggests a *quid pro quo*—do this and get that, as if God were a slot machine into which one pumps quarters until God is obliged to eventually pay out. You just don't know when or how much.

That, however, is not how God works. Such a god would be capricious, needy, and able to be bribed. "Give to get" suggests that God owes us something and will only provide if we do certain things. It removes God's sovereignty.

The people Malachi addressed were experiencing tough times—drought and scarcity. They were anxious and in their fear had stopped giving. All they could see was what they lacked. God promised if they were faithful in generosity, they would discover that there was already enough. The blessings were *already present*; they just needed to trust and share. Each giving an equal portion (a tithe) would assure none would be without.

You don't have to give to get. You can give *because you have already received.* You don't need to give something so that God will consider loving you, caring for you, or providing for you. It is the very nature of God to give. Your giving is a thankful response for what you already have received.

*For Focus and Reflection:* How does my giving reflect what I am most thankful for?

*Prayer: For your generosity that flowed from the first day of creation, I give you thanks. Amen.*

# Week 2 Going Deeper

**Resources for Individual Reflection or Group Discussion**

This week the focus included self-care and care for the gospel before finally opening up the conversation about money. While money is likely where you believed the topic would flow, does it surprise you that all of these other things are also about stewardship?

What does it mean to you to "offer your whole body as a living sacrifice?" If we understand ourselves as being of value to God, then it naturally follows that taking care of ourselves does matter. Take some time to analyze your sleep, exercise, and diet. Can you imagine tending to these things in a more disciplined and intentional manner as a spiritual act? Name one simple thing you can change in each of these three areas (sleep, exercise, diet) and find an accountability partner to keep you honest about your progress.

Think about ways your congregation might engage in disciplines related to self-care. Is there a walking group, yoga class, bicycling club, sports league, or other energetic activities that could provide elements of both self-care and fellowship? Can you see how doing things together can work toward mutual accountability and greater chance for success? It might be fun to host a contest related to healthy food, a sort of cook-off where folks can vote on their favorite dish. Maybe you can collect health-conscious recipes for a new kind of church cookbook! What kind of potluck supper theme could you create for fun and education?

**Read** Psalm 23. The author sees the provision of rest and safety as genuine conditions created by the presence of God. Where are your "quiet waters" and "green pastures"? Can you find more time to dwell in these spaces?

**Read** Matthew 28:19–20 and Luke 10:1–12. How do you

see yourself as a steward of grace as suggested in 1 Peter 4:10 (Day 10)? Is the good news about Jesus a treasure to be hidden, or shared? Can you tell your own faith story in an "elevator speech"? Do you understand that sharing your belief in Jesus is sharing grace with someone? How or why do you think this is so? Will you challenge yourself to talk more openly about your faith as a means of spreading grace in your community?

Can you imagine a way for your congregation to become more intentional about being stewards of grace? Are there opportunities to share stories (and to practice telling faith stories) and ways to invite others to your place of worship? Are you well-prepared to receive guests in everything from signage (how to find things) to being friendly with visitors (and not just each other)?

As we begin the money conversation, draft a short financial autobiography. List key moments in your life where you learned something significant about money. What was your first job? How much were you paid? What did you do with the money you earned? When did you start giving money to the church? How much did you give? How did you decide what the amount should be?

*For reading and further study: Unbinding the Gospel* by Martha Grace Reese; *Talking Faith* by Heather Kirk-Davidoff and Nancy Wood (both from Chalice Press); *God and Money* by Mark Allen Powell (Wm. B. Eerdmans Press).

*Going Deeper Still:* Complete a more detailed financial autobiography that traces your understanding of, and relationship with money across your lifetime. You can find a free tool at financialrecovery.com.

# DAY 15

• • • • • •

# Lusting for Money

*Lust for money brings trouble and nothing but trouble. Going down that path, some lose their footing in the faith completely and live to regret it bitterly ever after.* (1 Timothy 6:10, MSG)

It might surprise you to know that the Bible is relatively value neutral when it comes to wealth. Yes, there are plenty of warnings about the dangers of being rich, but in the end the Bible is less concerned about money than it is about what happens to us when we have it or when we don't. The money itself is not the issue—we are.

The passage above is often misquoted: "Money is the root of all evil". The problem is that money is *not* the root of all evil – "the *love* of money is the root of all kinds of evil" (NRSV). We don't need many stories to confirm the truth in that statement. We have all known people who, in the pursuit of wealth alone, have left a wake of disaster behind their choices. The same can be said of corporations that, in the sole interest of the bottom line, have made decisions that disrupt lives and even harm the environment. Any company that chooses a strategy where lawsuits related to harm caused are less expensive than fixing the problem falls into this category. Think Erin Brockovich.

When money alone becomes our desire, all other relationships suffer collateral damage, including our relationship with God. Wealth is like the splitting of the atom. Harnessed and contained it can power our homes. Unleashed without constraint, it can destroy our planet.

I particularly like *The Message* author Eugene Peterson's choice of *lust* over love in his translation because it suggests the corruption of something meant for good—a poignant and appropriate thought.

**For Focus and Reflection:** What one thing can I do today that shows money is not my true love?

**Prayer:** *In your mercy, help me to handle money with care. Amen.*

# Day 16

• • • • • •

# Realm Realities

*When did we ever see you hungry and feed you, thirsty and give you a drink? And when did we ever see you sick or in prison and come to you? ... Whenever you did one of these things to someone overlooked or ignored, that was me—you did it to me.'* (Matthew 25:37–40, MSG)

Here stewardship moves from the spiritual to the imminently practical. How exactly do you get to see the Realm of God? The steps are incredibly easy to follow: make certain that no one is without the basic means for human survival: food, water, clothing, physical wellness, and social justice. The combination is not only to be evidence of the Realm, but an actual experience of the Realm itself.

Beyond accountability for the well-being of others, stewardship is caring for the very person of Jesus. To fail to do these things not only abrogates a social contract but does violence to Jesus Himself. The record speaks for itself.

Aside from obvious social realities—when these things are present there is less crime, fewer incidents of violence, and a better, richer, and fuller sense of community—is the realization that this is what seems to matter to God. Your belief (or lack thereof) in any particular word or phrase within the Church's creeds (over which the faithful have bludgeoned one another for centuries) is not the question. It's doing, not dogma. Not simply right belief, but proper action.

Belief is not irrelevant. But what matters is whether or not that belief leads to making the world a better place for someone else. In the unique economy of God, improving another's life means improving your own simultaneously.

*For Focus and Reflection:* How can I help one person today with something they need to live?

*Prayer: Remind me, Holy One, that in giving to others, we truly receive for ourselves. Amen.*

# Day 17

• • • • • •

# Big Difference

*"There was a rich man who was dressed in purple and fine linen and who feasted sumptuously every day. And at his gate lay a poor man named Lazarus, covered with sores, who longed to satisfy his hunger with what fell from the rich man's table."* (Luke 16:19–20, NRSV)

In the ancient world if you had bread, you might be poor, but you were alive. If you had something to dip your bread in, you might be considered middle class. Add some meat, and you were upper crust. Have all of that *and* bread left over to clean your hands, and you were in the 1 Percent. Using bread as a napkin meant you were extraordinarily wealthy. Contrast that to Lazarus, who is hungry enough to want the rich man's napkin for supper. That is disparity.

As so often happens in Luke's Gospel, there is a sudden reversal of fortunes in the rest of Luke 16, so as to have the unnamed rich man in torment and Lazarus, the beggar, tucked in the bosom of Abraham. The rich man seeks relief, but there can be none. The die of the afterlife was cast in the current one. The rich man knew of Lazarus' need. In life he had it pretty good. Now in death, not so much, and Lazarus is finding comfort in the Father (Abraham) whose faith was counted as righteousness.

One is left to wonder: If the disparity in life had not been so great, would the disparity in death have been lessened as well? The rich man wants a warning for his family. Abraham says they have the Law and the Prophets. And if someone came back from the dead to tell them that treating the poor mattered, well, who would believe such a thing anyway?

***For Focus and Reflection:*** What is the legacy I am writing in my giving and living?

***Prayer:*** *For every time I have held my money tightly in the face of poverty, forgive me Lord. Amen.*

# Day 18

• • • • • •

# Foolish Stuff

*Take care! Be on your guard against all kinds of greed; for one's life does not consist in the abundance of possessions.* (Luke 12:15, NRSV)

I have nice stuff. I like my stuff. We had a flood and lost a lot of our stuff. But trust me, we still have plenty. I have a boat motor and it's a beauty—a 1955 Johnson 5 ½ horsepower that still purrs like a kitten. I should point out that I don't have a boat. I will probably never own a boat. But I have a motor. It is part of my stuff. And like it or not, my stuff defines me in a culture that views consumerism as a national virtue. Remember how we were told by the President, after 9/11, to go shopping. It's what we do. It's considered patriotic.

In Luke 12:13–21 Jesus tells the story of a man who hits the first century equivalent of the Powerball. He figures his future is secure. Build new, bigger barns, stash it all away, and then eat, drink, and be merry. No worries. Life is good.

If you remember the story, you know that on the very night he has planned his trip to the good life, Jesus says that an angel of the Lord appeared to him and called him a fool. Can you imagine? A fool. This said to a guy whose cattle and brokerage account are fat with all the financial resources he would ever need. He's no fool. He's to be admired. Right?

He is called a fool right before he learns that his life is required of him. And what of all his stuff? In the story all his conversations are monologues, no one else in the picture—not God, not community, not a single person to share with. When you tell it that way, it does seem kind of foolish.

*For Focus and Reflection:* Is there anything I have that could prove me to be the fool?

*Prayer: Keep me from playing the fool. Amen.*

# Day 19

• • • • • •

# Is Being Rich a Sin?

*"Do you have any idea how difficult it is for people 'who have it all' to enter God's kingdom? ... I'd say it's easier for a camel to go through a needle's eye than for the rich to get into God's kingdom."* (Mark 10:24, MSG)

Does Jesus have it in for the moneyed class? No, not really. He does care if we share when we have things, or covet others' success when we don't. Those behaviors build or undermine community. Good crops for a landowner meant more gleanings for the poor. Abundance for some meant more resources for all. In fact, to be rich was seen by some as a sign of blessing.

What more could there be to being righteous? Wealthy + Faithful = Blessed. That understanding is why the rich man in this story is so befuddled by his encounter with Jesus. He asks, "How do you get to heaven?" Jesus responds, "You need to give away your wealth to the poor so you will have treasure in heaven and follow me." The man is incensed at this, and goes away sad.

Jesus is inviting the man into discipleship—to follow *unreservedly*. In this case, the rich man's wealth is a stumbling block in his path. Jesus knows we can be tempted to rely on money more than God and that our wealth can insulate us from the plight of the poor. The Realm of God, which the rich man is being invited to glimpse, is a place where the poor are fed and cared for. The man's *divesting* of his wealth would be an *investment* in the Realm. He would be "all in." The text tells us "Jesus loved him." The results suggest the rich man loved his money more.

**For Focus and Reflection:** Do I own my stuff or does it own me?

**Prayer:** *Help me to invest more fully in the Realm of God. Amen.*

# Day 20

• • • • • •

# Harsh Words

*Will anyone rob God? Yet you are robbing me! But you say,*
*"How are we robbing you?" In your tithes and offerings!*
(Malachi 3:8, NRSV)

The Bible extends an invitation for us to live a certain way. When it comes to our money, it invites us to give a tithe. This is not for God, it is for us. It is for the benefit of the community. When we reject that invitation, there are consequences. The prophet equates the failure to give the 10 percent to a crime against God. In failing to protect and care for others via their offerings, the people have committed an affront to God. They have not been faithful to what God desires.

And so comes a word of judgment. It is issued upon those who "oppress the hired workers in their wages, the widow and the orphan, against those who thrust aside the alien, and do not fear me, says the Lord of hosts" (Malachi 3:5, NRSV). To not give generously is to deny God. It is to willfully ignore the safety net God has put in place to be sure that everyone has the basics for life. We are the very strands of fabric in that web of protection through our giving.

These days of prayer and reflection offer you a chance to measure your obedience and the benefit of your gifts not only to others but also to yourself. You may not be able to immediately achieve the high standard God sets for generosity, but you can commit yourself to growing toward what God desires. In so doing you can honor God and change the world. What we do with our money matters to God, and to us.

*For Focus and Reflection:* How am I also being robbed when I am not generous?

*Prayer: Lord, forgive me for withholding anything that belongs to you. Amen.*

# Day 21

• • • • • •

# Extravagant Generosity

*While [Jesus] was eating dinner, a woman came up carrying a bottle of very expensive perfume. Opening the bottle, she poured it on his head. Some of the guests became furious among themselves. "That's criminal! A sheer waste! This perfume could have been sold for well over a year's wages and handed out to the poor."* (Mark 14:3–5, MSG)

What would you give a year's salary for? You may be able to name a few things for yourself or your family, but can you imagine simply giving away an entire year's worth of earnings? That, and much more, is the value of the gesture the woman in this story makes.

What could prompt such an action? The account is told in all four gospels, each with a bit of variance. Only in John 12:1–8 is she named, Mary, and there we are to assume she is the sister of Lazarus, whom Jesus has raised from the dead. In the other three versions she is unnamed. In Luke, she is identified only as a harlot; in Matthew and Mark we know even less about her. The one detail they all agree on is the value of the ointment— and that she pours *all of it* on Jesus in an unprompted action of love and apparent gratitude.

If the value of the gift offered is to be understood in relationship to the depth of thanksgiving it represents, the story could be asking you to consider just how grateful you are for what you have received. When you consider your life with or without Jesus, how does the value of your offering reflect the profound nature of your appreciation for what God is doing in, through, and for you?

*For Focus and Reflection:* Does my life reflect what I am most grateful for?

*Prayer: God, may my gifts truly reflect the love I am receiving from you. Amen.*

# Week 3 Going Deeper

**Resources for Individual Reflection or Group Discussion**

In his book *Holy Currencies*, Eric Law suggests that "money was intended to be a temporary medium of exchange." At some point, we turned it into a commodity and stopped moving it as medium of exchange. Forgetting its original purpose has had devastating effects on human community.

This week as we turned our attention fully to the financial aspect of stewardship, things got a little rough! The selected texts called us out about harsh realities concerning our relationship with money and some of the dangers lurking in the shadows of this conversation.

The prophets of Israel (and in keeping with their tradition, Jesus) really do have a lot to say about the proper use of money. One can get the sense in the First Testament that if you want to know the spiritual condition of the nation, you look around at how many people are sleeping under bridges and eating out of dumpsters. In the Second Testament, for the Realm of God to be experienced the faithful must make it so by the proper employment of their resources, in full partnership with the Divine. In both Testaments, failure is not an option and comes with significant costs!

Can you think of ways you have spent money that in retrospect you might do differently if you had a "do-over"? Have you missed opportunities to have a positive moral influence with your money? Do you know of a person (or have you ever been that person) who put money ahead of relationships? Can you name some of the unintended consequences of doing this?

**Read** Luke 19:1–10. Legend has it that in the Middle Ages soldiers heading off to do battle in the Crusades would hold their sword hand up, out of the water, when being baptized. Allegedly, this permitted the hand to be used for killing, as it was not "buried with Christ." Some have mused that Christians in our consumer-driven economy do the same with their wallets! Christ can have all of us—except for our money! How does redemption function for Zacchaeus? Can/should such a transformation happen to us upon our decision to enter into the discipleship of Jesus? Why is it so difficult?

To take this conversation into our congregations, if our church budget really is a theological document, what does the church budget say about your priorities? Do the math. Divide your total operating receipts by the total spent on mission that does not directly benefit the membership. Are you a generous church? Do the same for your personal budget. Look at your total income (gross or net, we won't quibble here) and look at your total charitable spending. How are you doing? Can you find room for improvement? If your church decided to grow by 1 percent in its giving, what would that mean in your community, or for your denomination's mission work, in real dollars?

*For reading and further study: Holy Currencies* by Eric Law (Chalice Press); *Contentment in an Age of Excess* by Will Samson and Shane Claiborne (David C. Cook Publishing); *Enough* by Adam Hamilton (Abingdon Press).

*Going Deeper Still:* Read *The Steward: A Biblical Symbol Come of Age* by Douglas John Hall (Wm. B. Eerdmans Press).

# Day 22

· · · · · ·

# Let's Party!

*In the presence of the Lord your God...you shall eat the tithe of your grain, your wine, and your oil, as well as the firstlings of your herd and flock, so that you may learn to fear the Lord your God always.* (Deuteronomy 14:23, NRSV)

Most people know the meaning of tithe is 10 percent. In the Bible, it is understood to be 10 percent of your annual income, the yearly yield of the field. It didn't matter if the crops were good or bad, you brought in 10 percent of what you had produced. It was a pretty fair system.

What many people don't know is that the tithe, as described in Deuteronomy, was not a religious tax or legal obligation, but the fixings for a big old-fashioned potluck supper! Every year everyone came together to celebrate what the land had produced. You brought your tithe (or if it was too far to carry, the cash equivalent, which you converted to party supplies when you arrived) and you ate and drank together. In a subsistence economy, harvest and production were worthy of rejoicing!

Along with the music and dancing came the remembrance of a lasting Truth: God provides. Folks may have become excellent at farming and performed animal husbandry at a level that would earn a blue ribbon at the state fair. But when it was all said and done, after the seed was planted, only God could make it grow. And that is what is meant by "fear the Lord your God always." Remember, the source of your provision is not you. It is a providential gift from a loving Creator who gives in abundance all that is necessary for life.

***For Focus and Reflection:*** How can I celebrate God's generosity toward me today?

***Prayer:*** *Let my offerings be filled with joy and celebration for what you have given me. Amen.*

# Day 23

● ● ● ● ● ●

# Confessing Faith

*"A wandering Aramean was my ancestor; he went down into Egypt and lived there as an alien, few in number, and there he became a great nation mighty and populous. When the Egyptians treated us harshly and afflicted us... The Lord brought us out of Egypt with a mighty hand and an outstretched arm."* (Deuteronomy 26:5–8, NRSV)

The key moment of faith in the life of Israel is crossing the Red Sea. A former professor of mine liked to say the First Testament is written in both directions from Exodus 14:31. "Israel saw the great work that the Lord did against the Egyptians. So the people feared the Lord and believed in the Lord and in his servant Moses" (NRSV). It informs everything that precedes it and everything that follows it. It is Israel's salvation story.

It is not really a surprise then to find a retelling of this story connected to the annual gift of the tithe. The land, the resulting gift of that act of deliverance, has produced, and the people respond by making a gift (a tithe) from its abundance. As they offer the gift, they recite the story of their salvation. In generosity, everyone within the borders of the land is invited to the feast, even the stranger and the alien. There is enough for all. Everyone celebrates and everyone benefits. Israel remembers the source of its blessings.

Can you imagine saying, "I believe that Jesus is the Christ" when the plate is passed in worship? You may not be making a verbal confession, but you are saying something about what you believe and how deeply you believe it by the nature of (and your attitude about) your gift.

*For Focus and Reflection:* Are my gifts statements of doubt or faith?

*Prayer: Lord of deliverance, may my gifts reflect the grace I have received from your hand. Amen.*

# Day 24

• • • • • •

# Really?

*Toward evening the disciples approached him. "We're out in the country and it's getting late. Dismiss the people so they can go to the villages and get some supper." But Jesus said, "There is no need to dismiss them. You give them supper."* (Matthew 14:15–16, MSG)

In the story of the feeding of the 5,000, one crucial detail is often overlooked. When the disciples protest about the people's hunger, Jesus does not respond, "Stand back, I've got this." He doesn't reply with a pious, "God is in control and will provide." In every gospel account of this miracle, Jesus looks at the disciples and says, "You handle it." Really? Has Jesus been paying attention to their questionable competency on just about anything related to the Realm of God?

It is very important to note that the specific address to the disciples means that Jesus is talking to you, to me, to *us*. He is speaking to the *Church*. At one level that is unnerving. Really? You want us to take on a project like that? You're kidding, right? However, when we reflect on this phrase, it reminds us of the promise of Jesus that when the Holy Spirit comes, we too will be able to do the things Jesus has done—*even greater things,* he dares to say in the Gospel of John.

Jesus was in the business of making sure there was enough. Enough grace, enough healing, enough love, and even enough food. Wherever Jesus was, there was always enough. If you say that Jesus is in the church, well then, it is your business to be sure that there is enough. It's what Jesus does, and what he calls you to do. When the disciples gave what they had to Jesus, however insufficient it seemed, it was enough. Really!

*For Focus and Reflection:* Today, how can I be sure someone else has enough?

*Prayer: May I offer enough so that in your hands, it really is. Amen.*

# Day 25

• • • • • •

# Relief

*Regarding the relief offering for poor Christians that is being collected, you get the same instructions I gave the churches in Galatia. Every Sunday each of you make an offering and put it in safekeeping. Be as generous as you can. When I get there you'll have it ready, and I won't have to make a special appeal.* (1 Corinthians 16:1–3, MSG)

You might know it as *The Week of Compassion* or *One Great Hour of Sharing*. It may simply be called "Hurricane Relief," "Earthquake Assistance," or "Flood Fund." An offering received with the intent of helping people facing unimaginable challenges in the wake of a natural or human-created disaster. The need is obvious. The ask is clear. The response is to give.

The first such offering was received by Paul from the Mediterranean churches for the saints in Jerusalem. Folks who had nothing in common with one another, save one thing: Jesus. That was enough. Language, culture, custom, it didn't matter. A brother or sister in Christ was in need and that was reason enough to give.

How were folks to give? Generously. Paul defines generosity by pointing to the life of Jesus "who had the Realm of heaven but came to earth and yielded his life for us" (Philippians 2:8, author's translation). They were to give with joy! There was no pressure; the gift was voluntary. They were to give with faith! They could give, knowing that if they had a future need, God would provide for them the same way they were providing for those in Jerusalem. They were to give with discipline. The offering was not a last-minute action for which one was unprepared. On the contrary, it was an intentional action and one for which they were accountable.

*For Focus and Reflection:* Am I as prepared to give as I am to do other meaningful things?

*Prayer: When the moment of offering arrives, let me truly be prepared to give. Amen.*

# Day 26

● ● ● ● ● ●

# Gifted for Generosity

*We have gifts that differ according to the grace given to us: prophecy, in proportion to faith; ministry, in ministering; the teacher, in teaching; the exhorter, in exhortation; the giver, in generosity; the leader, in diligence; the compassionate, in cheerfulness.* (Romans 12:6–7, NRSV)

God's gifts given via the Holy Spirit are not superfluous. These gifts are given for the benefit of the Church, as a whole, to empower its witness and work in the world. They are grace-filled. They are of Divine origin. They matter.

Generosity is among the gifts God gives, that God enables, via the Holy Spirit. The Church needs great preaching and teaching; the faithful need to hear a prophetic word of challenge (prophecy does not necessarily mean "seeing the future"); people need compassion, care, and sound leadership. But in the end, what makes all this work is generosity. Yes, financial generosity empowers mission, so money is important. But so is the willing spirit to give one's whole self away to the project of being in true community. Give freely the best of whatever noble gift you have been given without reservation or thought of self-interest.

Paul also says that generosity is a fruit of the Spirit. The gifts may be particular, but the fruit is for everyone to bear: "the fruit of the Spirit is love, joy, peace, patience, kindness, generosity, faithfulness, gentleness, and self-control" (Galatians 5:22–23, NRSV). Reminiscent of Jesus' words about knowing trees by their fruit and people by their deeds, the meaning is clear: if you are walking in (with) the Spirit, there will be evidence of this in your life that others can see. And generosity is on the list.

*For Focus and Reflection:* What kind of fruit do people see in me by my giving?

*Prayer: May generosity hang from the branches of my life so that all may see I am rooted in your love. Amen.*

# Day 27

• • • • • •

# Being Church

*Now in Joppa there was a disciple whose name was Tabitha, which in Greek is Gazelle.\* She was devoted to good works and acts of charity. At that time she became ill and died. ... [Peter] turned to the body and said, "Tabitha, get up." Then she opened her eyes, and seeing Peter, she sat up.* (Acts 9:36–37, 40b, NRSV)

Tabitha is given the title "disciple." In other words, she is a follower of the way of Jesus who is to be counted equal to the men in the inner circle of leadership. Her story is a resurrection story. It manifests the power of Jesus at work via the Holy Spirit in the actions of the apostles. Jesus may have left the building, but his resurrection power is still at work. The raising of Tabitha is the proof.

It could have been anyone. Anyone could have been brought back to life if the only point of the story was the power of Jesus working to bring life out of death. But it wasn't just anyone. It was Tabitha. Her death had caused a crisis because there was apparently no one else to carry on her charitable work. The widows were depending on her, and her death brought grief and uncertainty.

This miracle is a statement that the God who calls for the care of the widows and orphans in the First Testament does nothing less in the Second. The Church, in order to be the Church, would need Tabitha, or more precisely would need to *be like* Tabitha, to be authentic and true to its calling. Generosity is both life-giving and life-preserving.

*For Focus and Reflection:* How can I be more of a disciple like Tabitha?

*Prayer: Help me to realize that being generous is what being the Church is all about. Amen.*

\*(Most versions translate this word "Dorcas." *Gazelle* is the author's choice.)

# Day 28

• • • • • •

# Total Transformation

*And all the believers lived in a wonderful harmony, holding everything in common. They sold whatever they owned and pooled their resources so that each person's need was met. They followed a daily discipline of worship in the Temple followed by meals at home, every meal a celebration, exuberant and joyful, as they praised God. People in general liked what they saw. Every day their number grew as God added those who were saved.* (Act 2:44–47, MSG)

When the Day of Pentecost comes, we find the disciples in an upper room. According to John 20:19 they were hiding—*locked* in with fear, *locked* up with silence, and *locked* out from changing their community. They are paralyzed from doing any sort of proclamation or good work.

But then the Holy Spirit arrives, and suddenly everything is different. They find their voice for telling the story of Jesus. They find the courage to do good works; believing that by sharing their resources they can eliminate *all* need within their community. And it works!

The Holy Spirit (which they have earnestly prayed for) gives them the power to tell the story of Jesus and to share in such a way as to provide everyone in the community with the basics for life. People on the *outside* find it compelling, and they want *in*. The disciples are worshiping God, doing evangelism, and practicing compassion—potent acts of stewardship—and the church grows.

This is the power of holistic stewardship. This is the real work of generosity. It changes you. It changes the world. It unlocks you from fear and anxiety and opens you up to the abundance and provision of God, which never fail.

*For Focus and Reflection:* What kind of gift would change me to be closer to the person I want to be?

*Prayer: As I prepare to make commitment to my congregation, let me do so with the belief that it will change me and the world in which I live. Amen.*

# Day 29

●●●●●●

# What Next?

*Stewardship is not fundraising! It is spiritual discipline – as important to your walk with Christ as prayer, worship, service, and study. To be a disciple is to be a steward.*

We started with Wow! We end with "What Next?" How do you go forward boldly into God's abundant world with confidence in God's provision? Will care for the earth become a consideration in your choices for consumption? Does the invitation to Sabbath rest urge you to explore its path to renewal and revitalization? Do you believe that caring for yourself is in fact a holy and blessed act that has the potential to enrich your community of faith as you express your gifts to their fullest? Has your vision and understanding of stewardship been enlarged beyond the church budget?

Stewardship is a journey, not a destination. It is a process that invites you to take stock of your entire life and respond with joy and thanksgiving for all that is in your sphere of influence. Stewardship is a commitment to a way of being in the world that recognizes the importance of managing well all that we have—not only for our benefit, but for the well-being of the whole of creation.

Above all stewardship is about joy. When you give your time, talent, and treasure to something you believe in, you feel joy when you see it succeed. So here is a challenge regarding your financial resources: Evaluate your current giving to things that matter and challenge yourself to grow by at least 1 percent a year, more when you are able. I promise you that both your delight and commitment to those causes will increase in direct proportion to your growth in generosity.

*For Focus and Reflection:* Does my commitment reflect my readiness for the stewardship journey?

*Prayer: May I find for myself, and share with others, the joy of generosity. Amen.*

35

# Week 4 Going Deeper

**Resources for Individual Reflection or Group Discussion**

Stewardship and the practice of generosity can bring great joy! In fact generosity is life-giving to both the giver and the recipient. However, it also is true that in our world and close at hand in our own neighborhoods, there are people in desperate need. So to simply proclaim God's abundance and to say that God will provide seem intellectually dishonest. If God's promise of provision were true, why do so many lack the essential things of life?

That, of course, is where the concept of being a steward takes on its deepest meaning for our time and place. God envisions us (in fact charges us) with being the source of that provision. The world as God imagines it is one of deep and abiding community where each individual is valued and loved by another in the same way that God loves and values us. In the First Testament, laws were established to make certain that no one was without the essentials. Even in the practice of borrowing and lending, a coat could not be held as collateral. It had to be returned to the borrower *each night* so that the one in debt had protection against the elements. The tithe itself was shared with the community, not only as a celebration, but as a hedge against life-threatening poverty.

We are very aware that the earth provides enough so that every person can have what they need for life. The problem is that we have arrived at a point where less than half the global population owns more than 50 percent of the global resources. This imbalance is growing, and without a sense of mutual accountability and responsibility, its effects could be devastating. The same is true for our natural resources of potable water, clean air, and tillable soil. Stewardship, the faithful and honest management of these things, is really the best hope the world has against the improper exploitation of God's people and creation. The stakes have never been higher and the urgency never greater. Being a faithful steward matters because you are an agent of hope, and a God-given solution to the crisis.

**Read:** Micah 6:1–5, 9–16. Can you see this as a consequence of failing to be a good steward? Can you name present-day accusations that God might make against us? Now read Micah 4:1–4, 6:6–8, and Isaiah 55. Do you see these as stewardship-related texts (or the result of stewardship well-practiced), given what we have explored the last 29 days? Name specific behaviors related to justice, mercy, and humility as they apply to stewardship in your life and in the life of your congregation. Hear God's affirmation in your life when you act in this way! See the blessing you become to the world.

In the end, some of us may feel that we don't have enough to give in order to make a difference in the face of great needs. We may feel we don't have anything to give at all. In the biblical understanding of community, it was understood that rich or poor—whether you had a little or a lot—you had something to give. The very act of giving something away shows that you have power over it and not the other way around. It also states that everyone matters in the community—everyone!

*Going Deeper Still:* Consider a careful evaluation of what you really have. Create a personal/family budget if you don't have one already. The point is both to have less anxiety about your finances and to build the capacity for generosity. Offer a personal finance class in your congregation. These resources may be helpful: *Money Sanity Solutions* by Nathan Dungan (Share, Save, Spend Publishing); *How to Be Rich* by Andy Stanley (Zondervan Publishing); *Loonie: Crazy Talk about Faith and Finances* by John VanDuzer (United Church Publishing House); *Making More With What You Have,* a video workshop by Bruce A. Barkhauer (centerforfaithandgiving.org/studyresources/personalfinancesworkshop).

# Congregational resources for Advent and Lent

## Partners in Prayer
Advent 2016
*Forum for Theological Exploration*
*Editors, Alisha L. Gordon & Cassidhe Hart*

This Advent, don't just light candles—ignite hearts. Imagine the voice of God taking on a new sound as robust and diverse as the world in which we live. Add the voices of the silenced and invisible to the Advent narrative of birth and the power of redemption to see the familiar tale in fresh, creative, and revolutionary stories of triumph and wonder. Written by a diverse group of the church's newest leaders, *Partners in Prayer 2016* will help you see the everyday incarnations of God among us, appearing in the midst of our struggles and celebrations.
9780827231412

## Fellowship of Prayer
Lent 2017
*Sharon Watkins and Rick Lowery*

Jesus' journey to the cross shows us the boldness of humility. From his ministry that taught us to view every person with love, hope, and value, to the criticisms of the imperial and societal powers that oppressed his people, to the sacrifice on Golgotha—every lesson from Christ teaches us humility and service to others. Join Sharon Watkins and Rick Lowery on a Lenten journey that will remind you of the role God calls us to play in the world.
9780827211148

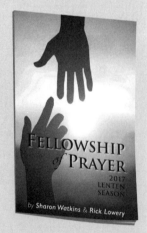

ChalicePress.com
1-800-366-3383

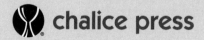 chalice press

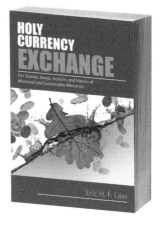
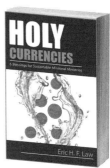

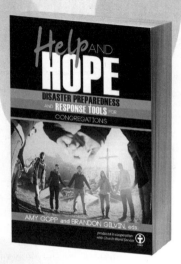